Alternative Energy
Solar Power

Capturing the Sun's Energy

LAURIE BREARLEY

Children's Press®
An Imprint of Scholastic Inc.

Content Consultant
Kevin Doran, J.D., Institute Fellow and Research Professor,
Renewable and Sustainable Energy Institute,
University of Colorado at Boulder

Library of Congress Cataloging-in-Publication Data
Names: Brearley, Laurie, 1953– author.
Title: Solar power : capturing the sun's energy / by Laurie Brearley.
Other titles: True book.
Description: New York, NY : Children's Press, [2018] | Series: A true book | Includes bibliographical
    references and index.
Identifiers: LCCN 2018009074| ISBN 9780531236864 (library binding) | ISBN 9780531239438 (pbk.)
Subjects: LCSH: Solar energy—Juvenile literature. | Power resources—Juvenile literature. | Clean energy
    industries—Juvenile literature.
Classification: LCC TJ810.3 .B7345 2018 | DDC 333.79/4—dc23 LC
record available at https://lccn.loc.gov/2018009074

All rights reserved. Published in 2019 by Children's Press, an imprint of Scholastic Inc.
Printed in China 62

SCHOLASTIC, CHILDREN'S PRESS, A TRUE BOOK™, and associated logos are trademarks and/or
registered trademarks of Scholastic Inc.

Scholastic Inc., 557 Broadway, New York, NY 10012

1 2 3 4 5 6 7 8 9 10 R 28 27 26 25 24 23 22 21 20 19

**Front cover: Crescent Dunes Solar
Energy Facility in Nevada**
Back cover: Solar panels in South Africa

Find the Truth!

Everything you are about to read is true *except* for one of the sentences on this page.

Which one is **TRUE**?

T or F   Solar power can help make salt water drinkable.

T or F   The sun lies about 500 million miles (805 million kilometers) from Earth.

Find the answers in this book.

Contents

1 Our Star

What are some ways people can
use energy from the sun?. 9

2 From Solar Energy to Electricity

Which methods are used to turn
solar energy into usable electricity? 19

THE BIG TRUTH!

Solar Power in Space

How does the International
Space Station get its
power? 28

Astronaut

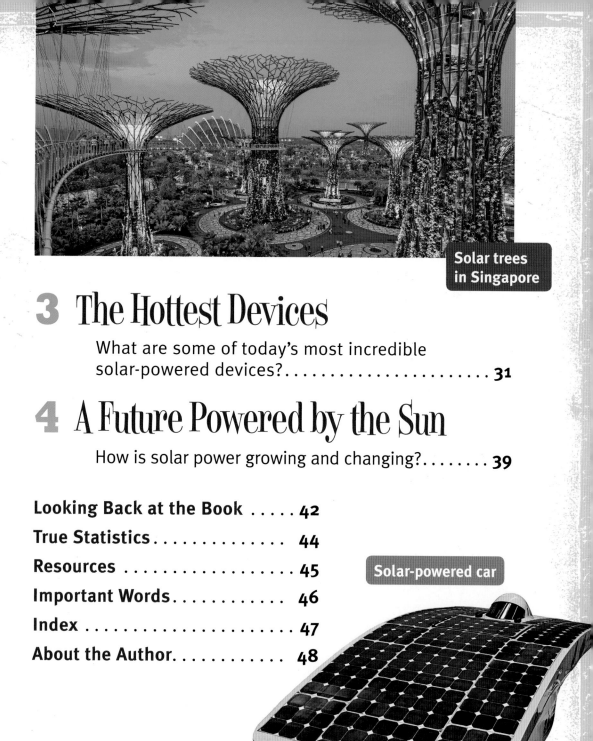

Solar trees in Singapore

Solar-powered car

A Need for Alternative Energy

We use energy every day. It fuels cars and powers cell phones. It cools homes when it's hot outside and warms them when the weather turns cold. It provides light through the night while the sun shines on the other half of the world.

All this energy must come from somewhere. Since the 1700s, people have relied mostly on **fossil fuels** such as coal, oil, and natural gas. These materials burn easily to create heat and can be turned into electricity. But they are far from perfect.

Our supply of fossil fuels is limited. Experts predict that **fossil fuels will dwindle and their cost will rise**. In addition, **burning these fuels releases harmful substances**.

Some substances trap heat within the **atmosphere**, leading to **climate change**. Others cause health problems, including heart and lung diseases.

What Can We Do?

Experts around the world are working on safer, healthier, and renewable alternatives to fossil fuels. The best replacements would serve the world's energy needs without damaging the planet or us.

Turn the page and learn the secrets of one of these alternative energies: solar power.

The sun supplies Earth with more energy each hour than all of the planet's people use in a year.

CHAPTER 1

Our Star

About 93 million miles (150 million kilometers) away from our planet, a massive ball of hydrogen, helium, and other materials burns at an incredibly high temperature. This is the brightly shining star we call the sun. The sun is located at the center of our solar system. It is like a huge furnace. The burning of its gases gives off a tremendous amount of energy. This energy escapes into outer space in all directions. Some of it reaches Earth.

Light and Heat

Energy from the sun reaches Earth's surface in the form of light. This light provides us with heat. Since the earliest days of civilization, humans have used solar energy for its light and heat. The energy of the sun also helps plants grow and keeps animals alive.

Timeline of Solar Energy

1839
French scientist Edmond Becquerel discovers the photovoltaic effect, the creation of electrical current in certain materials when they are exposed to sunlight.

1954
A team of researchers unveils the first practical solar cell technology.

1839 ▸ **1941** ▸ **1954** ▸ **1956–1957**

1941
Engineer Russell Ohl invents the solar cell.

1956–1957
The first office building to be heated entirely by passive and active solar energy is built in Albuquerque, New Mexico.

For centuries, scientists and engineers have worked to create new technology for capturing the energy of the sun and converting it into useful heat or electricity. At present, both are being done, and new breakthroughs are being made all the time. But there is still a lot left to learn.

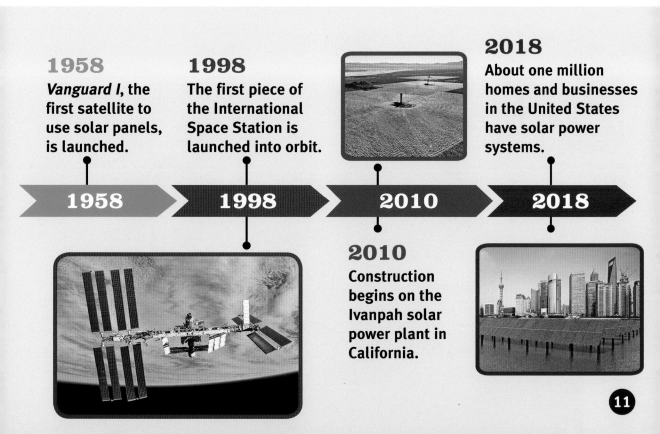

1958
Vanguard I, the first satellite to use solar panels, is launched.

1998
The first piece of the International Space Station is launched into orbit.

2018
About one million homes and businesses in the United States have solar power systems.

1958 1998 2010 2018

2010
Construction begins on the Ivanpah solar power plant in California.

Obstacles to Overcome

Earth receives more than enough solar power to serve all our energy needs. But the nature of sunlight makes capturing solar power a complicated process. Sunlight scatters widely, so it must be gathered and concentrated. Its energy is also blocked from reaching the surface of Earth during cloudy weather and at night. For this reason, solar energy is often stored for use during these times.

In many remote villages around the world, solar power is the cheapest, most reliable source of energy available.

The Greenhouse Effect

The heat rays of the sun break through the air and warm the planet's surface during the day. This heat energy is trapped by Earth's atmosphere, the layers of gases surrounding the planet. The atmosphere keeps the heat from escaping into space too quickly. At night, the heat absorbed during daylight keeps temperatures from getting too cold. This process is called the greenhouse effect. It is what keeps our planet warm enough to sustain life.

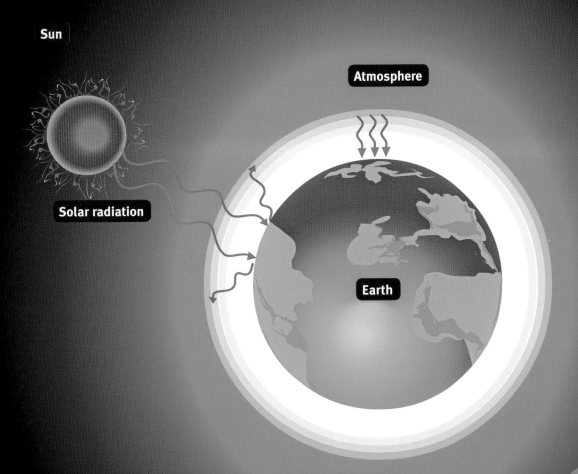

Sun

Atmosphere

Solar radiation

Earth

Heating Buildings

The sun's energy can be used to heat buildings without using up other fuels. There are two basic types of solar heating systems: passive and active. In passive systems, the building itself is designed to naturally distribute the sun's light and heat throughout. A number of design elements can help maximize the sun's heat. Furniture, walls, and floors absorb and store heat during the day. At night, they slowly release the heat to keep the building warm.

Houses with passive solar systems often feature steep roofs and projecting windows.

In active systems, solar energy is collected with special devices and then pumped through the building. It can be set up in several

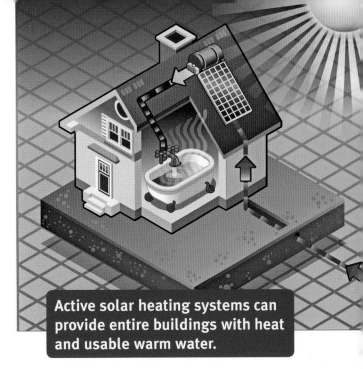

Active solar heating systems can provide entire buildings with heat and usable warm water.

ways. In one of them, a solar heating device is placed on the roof of a house. It is made of three layers: clear glass or plastic on top, a black panel in the center, and **insulation** underneath. Sunlight shines through the clear top, and the black panel absorbs the heat. The insulation keeps heat from escaping. Water passes through tubes in the device, absorbing the trapped heat. Pumps then **circulate** the warm water through pipes in the building.

Solar stills are designed to be portable so people can carry them when traveling to remote areas.

From Salt Water to Fresh Water

Solar energy can also be used to create clean drinking water. There is so much salt in ocean water that humans cannot drink it safely. However, a device called a solar still can make even the saltiest water drinkable. Salt water is added to a black pan and covered with a glass cone. Sunlight shines through the cone, **evaporating** the water and leaving the salt behind. The water **condenses** on the inside of the cone and trickles down. Fresh, drinkable water collects in containers at the edges of the still.

Solar Cooking

Devices called solar cookers can cook food and boil water. Because they require no wood, gas, or other fiery fuel, they are useful where such resources are scarce. In tropical countries, for example, firewood is often in short supply. Instead, these cookers can be used to prepare almost any dish that would be cooked over a fire. A solar cooker surrounds a pot or pan with reflective surfaces. These surfaces focus the sunlight, heating anything inside the cooker. Today, scientists continue to invent new and more complex methods for using solar energy.

Almost any kind of food can be prepared in a solar cooker.

The Ivanpah solar power plant in California provides energy to about 140,000 homes in the state.

CHAPTER 2

From Solar Energy to Electricity

While solar energy can be used in many different ways, perhaps its most exciting purpose today is as a source of electricity. To turn sunlight into usable electricity, we rely on small devices called solar cells. Solar cells are also called photovoltaic (foh-toh-vul-TAY-ik) cells. *Photo* refers to the Greek word for "light." *Voltaic* comes from "volt," a unit of electrical power.

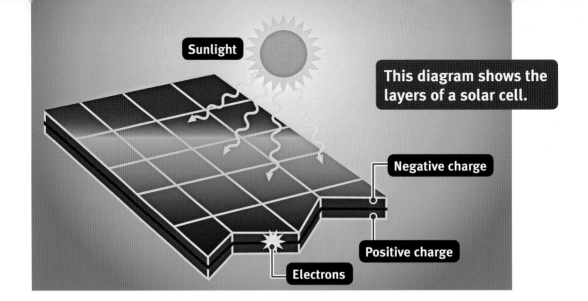

Sunlight

This diagram shows the layers of a solar cell.

Negative charge

Positive charge

Electrons

How Solar Cells Work

A solar cell is a thin, wafer-like device. It is made of two layers of material that can **conduct** electricity. The top layer has a negative charge. This means it has extra **electrons** in its atoms. The bottom layer has a positive charge. This means it has empty spaces where electrons could fit. When sunlight hits the top layer, electrons shake loose. This creates electricity. The loose electrons are attracted to the empty spaces in the bottom layer. This makes the electricity flow.

Sometimes solar cells are connected directly to an electrical device. At other times, they are connected to batteries that store the electricity for later. While solar cells vary in size, they are generally quite small. They do not create much electricity on their own. This means that many cells often need to work together to generate a useful amount of electricity. A device made up of multiple solar cells is called a solar panel.

The average solar panel measures about 65 inches (165 centimeters) by 39 inches (99 cm), but some are much larger.

Solar Electricity at Work

Photovoltaic cells can be used to power electrical devices of all sizes. Small handheld objects such as watches or calculators can be powered effectively using just a few tiny solar cells. Larger devices such as lawn mowers and refrigerators need more solar cells to be able to function.

Solar panels are the perfect power source for space exploration vehicles such as this Mars rover.

Large solar panels are needed to power buildings or other large structures. For example, solar panels often generate and store power for the lights that brighten billboards through the night. They are also used to power lighthouses by the sea. Homeowners can install solar panels on the outside of their houses. If

Solar lighthouses absorb sunlight during the day and light up at night so ships can safely navigate around dangerous coastlines.

the panels produce more electricity than the house needs, the extra can be sent back on to the power grid and used to power other homes. The power company can then pay homeowners for providing extra power to the grid.

Solar Panels Everywhere

In crowded cities, it is not always easy to find space for solar panels. To deal with this issue, engineers have found creative ways to place panels in busy areas. For example, solar panels can be placed above parking lots. Some towns have also placed panels into bike paths and sidewalks. There are even shingles made of solar panels. People can cover their roofs in these shingles instead of mounting larger panels to their homes.

Parking beneath solar panels keeps cars from getting hot in the sun. Meanwhile, the panels collect energy to power the parking lot's lights.

Some solar arrays, such as this one in Shanghai, China, are built offshore, where they will not take up valuable space on land.

Solar Arrays

Sometimes even a large solar panel is not quite enough when a lot of electricity is needed. Multiple solar panels can then be combined into a solar **array**. Solar arrays can help provide power to remote areas. These stand-alone systems can attach directly to a water pump or a series of streetlamps. They may also power homes, schools, or hospitals. One day soon, solar arrays might even be able to power entire cities.

Each of the towers at California's Ivanpah solar power plant is taller than the Statue of Liberty.

Concentrated Solar Power

Photovoltaic cells aren't the only way to turn solar energy into electricity. Another method relies on something called concentrated solar power. The world's largest concentrated solar power plant is the Ivanpah solar plant, located in the Mojave Desert in California. At this plant, there are three huge towers. Thousands of mirrors are arranged around each tower. They reflect sunlight toward the towers. Inside the towers are tubes filled with fluid. The fluid absorbs the sun's heat, creating steam. The steam powers **generators** to make electricity.

Concentrated solar power systems can also be arranged in other ways. The mirrors in **trough** systems are U-shaped and set up in long lines. A fluid-filled pipe runs along the middle of the mirrors. The U shape of the mirrors reflects the heat of the sun onto the pipe, heating the oil or liquid salt inside to temperatures as high as 735 degrees Fahrenheit (390 degrees Celsius). The hot oil is pumped into a separate system where it boils water to create steam. This steam powers a generator.

Workers assemble curved mirrors for a concentrated solar power system.

Solar Power in Space

The International Space Station (ISS) zooms around Earth 220 miles (354 km) above the surface. The ISS is a huge spacecraft where astronauts can live for months at a time. The astronauts conduct experiments to study the effects of outer space on the human body and to devise ways to improve space travel. The ISS is packed with advanced technology. Many of its functions rely on electricity. But where does the electricity come from as the station floats in space? The sun!

The ISS has four sets of solar arrays. Together, they are roughly the size of a football field.

Each array has thousands of solar cells that convert sunlight directly into electricity.

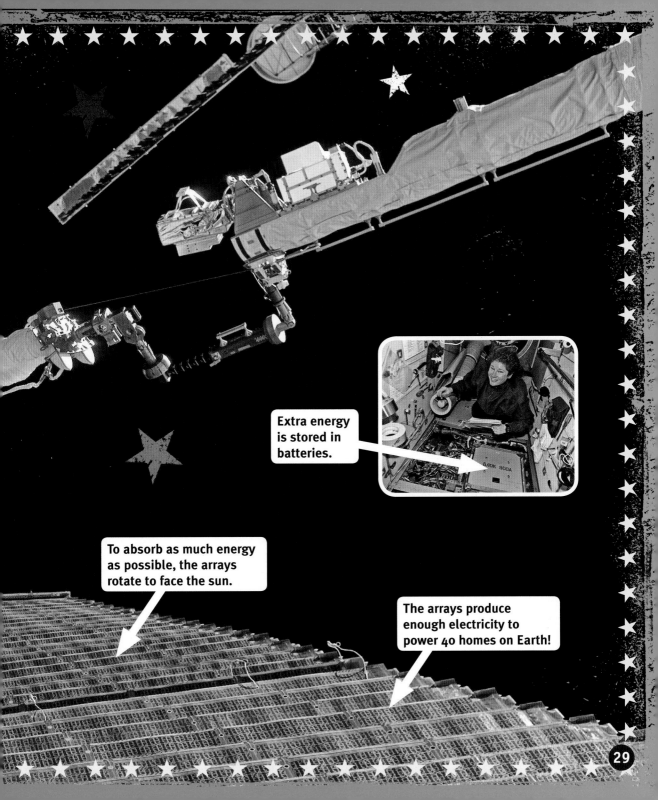

Extra energy is stored in batteries.

To absorb as much energy as possible, the arrays rotate to face the sun.

The arrays produce enough electricity to power 40 homes on Earth!

Arizona's Maricopa Solar Plant began operating in 2010, making it the country's first commercial solar power plant.

SunCatcher dishes reflect sunlight onto a receiver that collects heat and uses it to power a generator.

The Hottest Devices

Today, solar power supplies less than 1 percent of the world's energy. But this is rapidly changing. Between 2015 and 2016, the use of solar power grew by roughly 50 percent—faster than any other type of energy. More people around the world see solar power as a promising alternative energy. This interest is driving improvements in technology, and researchers are finding many new and incredible ways to use the sun's energy.

The weather in Singapore is often very hot. The solar trees in Gardens by the Bay are designed to absorb heat, cooling the park and making it more comfortable for visitors.

A New Type of Tree

It takes a lot of electricity to power a large, busy city. There are countless lights, buildings, and other systems that require power to work. Figuring out ways to decrease the use of fossil fuels in big cities will go a long way toward making the planet a greener place. Solar power could play a major role in this effort. In Singapore, a large Southeast Asian city, creative engineers have found a new way to gather solar power.

Like many city parks, Singapore's Gardens by the Bay is filled with trees. But these aren't just any trees. They are made of steel and concrete, and they have solar panels and lights installed on them. During the day, the trees collect solar energy. At night, this energy powers the trees' lights, creating a beautiful place to enjoy the outdoors. It also powers the park's greenhouses, where hundreds of thousands of plants from around the world grow.

The huge greenhouses at Gardens by the Bay receive energy from the nearby solar trees. They also rely on passive heating from sunlight to provide a warm environment for rare plants.

Solar Impulse 2 flies above the Golden Gate Bridge in San Francisco as part of its record-setting trip around the world.

Flight Powered by Sunlight

In 2016, Swiss pilots Bertrand Piccard and Andre Borschberg completed a flight all the way around the world. Their plane, *Solar Impulse 2*, flew nearly 25,000 miles (40,234 km) using no fuel but the sun. It was the first time a solar-powered plane had flown such a long distance. Because the plane only had room for one person at a time, Piccard and Borschberg took turns in the cockpit as it made stops around the world.

Most airplanes burn huge amounts of fossil fuels to power their massive engines. This releases a great deal of pollution into the air. But *Solar Impulse 2* didn't need any fossil fuels at all. Instead, its wings were covered with more than 17,000 solar panels. The panels charged the plane's batteries, allowing it to keep flying even in the dark. Piccard and Borschberg hope their flight will inspire more people to use solar power and other renewable energies instead of fossil fuels.

Pilot Bertrand Piccard takes a selfie while flying *Solar Impulse 2* from Oklahoma to Pennsylvania.

A Wheel That Eats Garbage

A lot of trash ends up floating in the waters of the Inner Harbor in Baltimore, Maryland. One Baltimore resident found a way to help solve this issue using solar energy. He built a solar-powered water wheel that lifts trash out of the water and onto a conveyor belt. The belt takes the trash to a nearby dumpster. The wheel has been such a success that other cities around the world have contacted its inventor to ask for tips on cleaning up the trash in their own waterways.

Inventor John Kellett created the Inner Harbor Water Wheel.

Conveyor belt

Wheel

Home Away from Home

A company called Nice Architects has created a portable home called an Ecocapsule. Each Ecocapsule is powered entirely by solar and wind power. About the size of a car, it has a sleeping space, lights, and even a small kitchen area inside. Because it is so small and does not require any fuel, it can be placed almost anywhere on Earth. Travelers can have a comfortable place to sleep even when visiting the world's most remote locations!

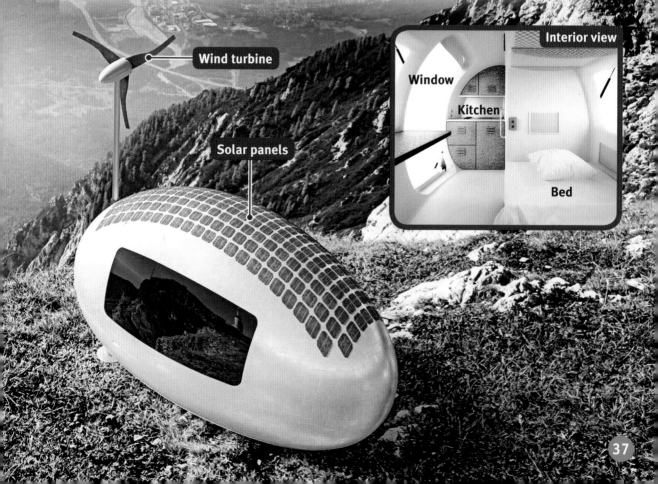

Wind turbine

Solar panels

Interior view

Window

Kitchen

Bed

At the U.S. Department of Energy's annual Solar Decathlon event, teams of college students compete to build the most effective solar-powered homes.

A Future Powered by the Sun

As solar energy technology becomes more powerful and less expensive to install, its use will become even more widespread. If the growth of solar power continues at its current rate, it could one day provide most of the electricity used on Earth. It could play a role in almost every part of our lives. Soon, almost everyone could have solar-powered homes, cars, and much more. Solar power can drive us into the future!

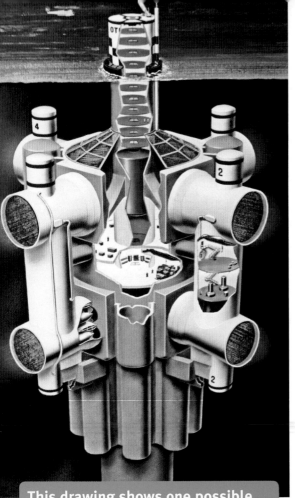

This drawing shows one possible design of a device that would collect solar energy from the ocean.

Power from the Sea

Covering roughly 70 percent of the planet, the ocean naturally absorbs a lot of solar energy. Researchers are working on ways to use this energy. One possible system would rely upon the surface waters that are warmed by sunlight. Their warmth would heat a special fluid that boils at low temperatures. The fluid turns to steam, which would power a generator. Then it would flow through tubes in deeper, cold water to cool into a liquid so it could be used again.

Solar Movers

Researchers are also using solar cells to power vehicles. In the American Solar Challenge, college and university teams from around the world design, build, and race solar-powered cars. Teams drive up to 2,000 miles (3,219 km) on highways and roads, facing all kinds of weather. They must design fast, efficient cars to win. The discoveries these students make could one day be used to build the everyday cars that most people drive. They could help create a greener world powered with solar energy! ★

Students from McGill University assemble their solar-powered car during the American Solar Challenge race.

Looking Back at the Book

What have you learned? Here's a quick review!
Can you add any details to the bits and pieces below?

PAGES 8–10

What creates solar power?

★ **The sun**

PAGE 19

What does *photovoltaic* mean?

★ *photo* = "light," from Greek
★ *voltaic* = "volt," a unit of electrical power

PAGES 14–17

Uses for solar heat

Heat and cool homes

Separate salt from salt water

Cook food

Ways to turn solar energy into electricity

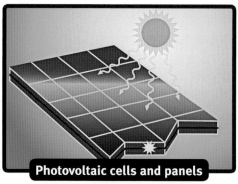
Photovoltaic cells and panels

Concentrated solar power systems

Solar-powered devices

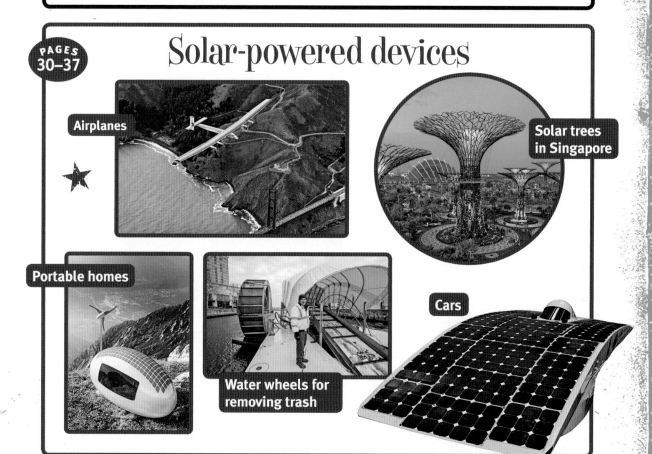

Airplanes

Solar trees in Singapore

Portable homes

Water wheels for removing trash

Cars

Distance from Earth to the sun: About 93 million mi. (150 million km)

Largest solar power plant by size: Ivanpah in California (1,000 acres, or 405 hectares)

Number of photovoltaic cells in a typical solar panel: 60 to 72

Number of photovoltaic cells powering the International Space Station: 262,400

Number of U.S. homes and businesses with solar energy systems: About 1 million

Number of people in the United States who worked in the solar power industry as of 2016: Nearly 260,000

Did you find the truth?

T Solar power can help make salt water drinkable.

F The sun lies about 500 million miles (805 million kilometers) from Earth.

Resources

Books

Bang, Molly. *Buried Sunlight: How Fossil Fuels Have Changed the Earth.* New York: The Blue Sky Press, 2014.

Otfinoski, Steven. *Wind, Solar, and Geothermal Power: From Concept to Consumer.* New York: Children's Press, 2016.

Sneideman, Joshua. *Renewable Energy: Discover the Fuel of the Future With 20 Projects.* White River Junction, VT: Nomad Press, 2016.

Taylor-Butler, Christine. *The Sun.* New York: Children's Press, 2014.

Vogel, Julia. *Solar Power.* Ann Arbor, MI: Cherry Lake Publishing, 2013.

Waxman, Laura Hamilton. *Exploring the International Space Station.* Minneapolis: Lerner Publications, 2012.

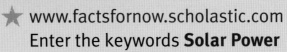

Visit this Scholastic website for more information on Solar Power:
★ www.factsfornow.scholastic.com
Enter the keywords **Solar Power**

Important Words

array (uh-RAY) an object made up of a large number of smaller objects

atmosphere (AT-muhs-feer) the mixture of gases that surrounds a planet

circulate (SUR-kyuh-late) to move in a circle or pattern

climate change (KLYE-mit CHAYNJ) global warming and other changes in the weather and weather patterns that are happening because of human activity

condenses (kuhn-DENS-iz) changes from a gas or vapor into a liquid

conduct (kuhn-DUHKT) to allow heat, electricity, or sound to travel through

electrons (i-LEK-trahnz) tiny, negatively charged particles that move around the nucleus, or center, of an atom

evaporating (i-VAP-uh-rate-ing) changing into a vapor or gas

fossil fuels (FAH-suhl FYOO-uhlz) coal, oil, or natural gas, formed from the remains of prehistoric plants and animals

generators (JEN-uh-ray-turs) machines that produce electricity by turning a magnet inside a coil of wire

insulation (in-suh-LAY-shuhn) material that helps stop heat, electricity, or sound from escaping

trough (TRAWF) a long, narrow container

Index

Page numbers in **bold** indicate illustrations.

About the Author

Laurie Brearley has written and edited numerous children's books and articles on a wide range of topics in science and social studies. She holds degrees from the University of New Hampshire and Boston University. Brearley believes that learning is a lifelong pursuit. She currently lives in Binghamton, New York, and is proud to be a descendant of David Brearley, one of the signers of the U.S. Constitution.